Bear Lexicon

Bear Lexicon

Eric Fisher Stone

Clare Songbirds
Publishing House

Clare Songbirds Publishing House Poetry Series
ISBN 978-1-957221-13-7
Clare Songbirds Publishing House
Bear Lexicon© 2023 Eric Fisher Stone

Printed in the United States of America
FIRST EDITION

140 Cottage Street
Auburn, New York 13021
www.claresongbirdspub.com

The insects parted with their names in vast clouds and swarms of ephemeral syllables buzzing and stinging and humming and flitting and crawling and tunnelling away.

As for the fish of the sea, their names dispersed from them in silence throughout the oceans like faint, dark blurs of cuttlefish ink, and drifted off on the currents without a trace.

—Ursula K. Le Guin, "She Unnames Them."

Being called, hearing oneself being named, receiving a name for the first time involves something like the knowledge of being mortal and even the feeling that one is dying.

—Derrida, *The Animal That Therefore I Am*

Acknowledgements

Beyond Words: Worm Saviors
Bombfire: Verses from Elmer, Let There Be Light, Frog in Amber
Catamaran Literary Reader: Before Naming
Cider Press Review: Dirt Ecstasies
Circle Show: Dear Razorback Musk Turtle
Clade Song: Ode to Rats
Coachella Review: Bear Lexicon
Concho River Review: The Feral Child's Ecstasy
Cypress: The Ecstasy of Owls
Fahmidan: A Billion Heartbeats
Grim & Gilded: Monsters
Gyroscope Review: The Fermi Paradox
Jalmurra: Galileo, Voyage to Pluto
Last Stanza Poetry Journal: Becoming the Song, The Big Dipper,
        Philosophy is Preparation for Death
Neologism Poetry Journal: The Lake Worth Child,
        Clownfish in Love with the Moon,
        A Garden Slug has 27,000 Microscopic Teeth
North of Oxford: Javelina Aubade, The Immanence of God,
        Bullfrog Witness
Red Planet Magazine: Ohthere the Astronaut
Sky Island Journal: Life Stew, If the Moon Were Human
Thimble Magazine: Adam Means Red Earth
Third Wednesday: Beasts Naming
Adam Trouvaille Review: Ghost Tracks
West Trade Review: The Making, Deer Skull, Love Song to a
        Harvest Mouse, Elegy for the Ivory-Billed Woodpecker
Willawaw Journal: Meeting a Cottonmouth
Willows Wept Review: Deer Shall Inherit the Earth, Stray Cat
Wine Cellar Press: Arachnophilia
Words & Whispers: Thanatophobia

Contents

Part I

Bear Lexicon

What can be shown, cannot be said.
—Wittgenstein, Tractatus

His parents stepped off the trail
to film a moose. Next dawn no one found
the child except a grizzly sow.

She lost a cub that spring, nursed
the three-year-old, milk thundering
from her nipples' dark gourds, his mouth

juiced with butterfat thick as moonlight.
Midsummer, he forgot human speech
while his surviving cub sister chewed

raw salmon, their stomachs packing
fetid meat, raspberries' lacquer gushing
their teeth scarlet. By autumn

he mimicked bear huffs and grunts
as wind sluiced pines, chipmunks hurtled
like mad rats through woods without words

for death. The boy died that winter
in the hibernating den. Mother bear's
bready hump slurred warm with her pulse.

His last wordless thoughts seemed: *Here,*
the ground creams snow. My ear pressed
to her back gathers her sound.

My breath walks through the cold air.
Above, the world tastes like trees. Here
is earth. I love what I cannot name.

Before Naming

*And Adam gave names to all cattle, and to the fowl of
the air, and to every beast of the field.*
—Genesis, 2:20, KJV

Puffing labels for bird, horse
and serpent, Adam's tongue tilled
meaning from mystery. Before words,

ants kissed pheromones, amoebas
seeped like scrambled eggs, frogspawn
spumed tadpoles without phrases for water,

star, God. Pterodactyl angels
ripped hazards through skies, this same air,
this soil, raw as a newborn's first milk

which can't be spoken, only tasted.
Dragonflies mated over the plunder
of slime when lightning startled Earth

with amazement hotter than knowledge.
From throaty plugging to lipping trills,
we jail the world in our mouths. The bird

doesn't sort horse from hippo, snake from snail.
She sings of cherries lush as almonds,
the electric sky tanged with her voice.

A Blind and Deaf Dog

Haystacks bite my fur, earth melded to one smell
of light honeyed with grasshopper legs.
I woke smashed by a truck
and could no longer see, my vision
a black halo blinding the sun from my brain,
molasses-sweet shade spilling power
in my mouth. Born deaf,
the rabbit thumps my ears' runnels
to a void where the farmer's call drowns
with the dawn-yawp of roosters.

I taste Herefords bawling
their breath's misty choirs,
bestial angels chanting psalms
of corn and grass, the universe
singing against my paws
as I lick all names like braille,
words made flesh; I am speaking.

The Immanence of God

Harvester ants boiled from red mounds
like witches' venomous breasts.
Texas pastures plumed bluebonnets
to the back of Grandpa's land, a creek bed
where water moccasins opened

the fatal flowers of their mouths.
The thicket guarded an enchanted kingdom.
Ogres and dragons lumbered
past chicken coops, the shed we saw
through briars clearly inhabited

by green gnomes with juniper beards.
Thorns jammed the jade-leaved threshold
to the other world. Gnat-clogged skies,
earth lubed with snails wouldn't satisfy
our lust for fantasy. Later I realized

specks of dust are planets whirring
in shafts of light, those trees weren't borders
to the sublime but the sublime itself.
Wild plums blister sweetness
on the only world where love is real.

Frog in Amber

In Myanmar, 2018, a 99-million-year-old frog was
found trapped in amber with its potential last meal,
a beetle. The Cretaceous period amphibian lived
contemporary with dinosaurs.

When the pine wept
syrupy resin, her tears
gummed me to death
with gold, my flesh glassed

in this bullion glacier.
My webbed hands tried
to swim the candled slurry
until I became a runestone

casting scientific magic,
to call stegosaur gods
for truth and company.
My cocoon's caramel speaks

mysteries curators read
and cannot understand:
forests with unnamed smells,
rituals of trilobites and snails.

Do humans know the sound
of my trilling chin's love-croak,
the taste of my last beetle?
Are my pleasures lost to time

as yours will? I sleep
in this hunk of sap, waiting
for your vision to wake me
and imagine my sipping breath.

First Love

Museum air conditioners wafted dust.
Other second graders oohed
at stegosaur bones while I gazed
into a giant human cell.

Plastered above, her cratered lake
glimmered like a jellyfish
in the marble room. In love
with the replica, I still speak to her.

Seduce me your round body,
undress your white earth, juicy pearl,
apple flesh, fragrant planet,
warm carnation, milk-glutted breast.

Mitochondria heats your pale city.
Your nucleus weaves tenderness
and genes, goddess egg, your spell book
kindling all life with sentences

written in a double helix.
Feeding sugars to your trillion selves,
when I weep or laugh, I forget
your kisses puckered inside me.

Javelina Aubade

Javelina (Tayassu tajacu) also known as collared peccary, are medium-sized animals that look similar to a wild boar. They have mainly short coarse salt and pepper colored hair, short legs, and a pig-like nose.
—Arizona-Sonora Desert Museum

Chomping prickly pear, cholla spines
in ripping kisses, you clop earth
with your hooves' tender bells.

Sauntering campgrounds, your snout
delights at the dirt's pungent nest
when dawn splits through mesas.

I love your humid musk, your crescent moon
circling your neck, your rage snarling
with teeth that could tear my tendons.

Rain gorges the ground, creosote
perfumes laughing toads when you funnel
the world's voluptuous juices

into your mouth, your joy buoyant
as coconuts. I take your picture
and wave goodbye, my hooved love,

huffing hedgehog, silver jackfruit,
mesquite marauder, milking the plunder
of nopal. Alone, nightly in bed,

I conjure your oval bulk and taste
your absence in the dark, grieving
that wild javelinas live no longer

than ten years and you might have died.
Your bread loaf shape leaps naked
in the wind, so happy, and free.

Ode to Rats

I think rats are tender
as loaves of bread. Pattering cupboards,
their ballpoint pink noses
shiver with fruity pleasure.

Leaping through gardens, they chew
grasshoppers or crisps of okra.
Woodpile gnomes, sewer goblins,
I admire their dashing pills.

Their whiskers sweep alleys
like blind wizards nibbling runic crumbs.
Lab rats average over 10 ounces,
the weight of a human heart.

Some say people should be warriors
and chuck pity for power. I say
the world is nursed by the softness of rats
I love more than my eyes.

Monsters

Siehst, Vater, du den Erlkönig nicht?
—Goethe, *The Elf King*, put to music by Schubert

Few daylit monsters appear. They hulk
between owls' swirling wings and treble doves
at dawn. Most nightmares I wander streets
where fog smells like hot licorice.

Sometimes the Elf King's knifing fingers fasten
my neck. Sometimes the sun craters
into earth; an engorged blister of light
crisps downtown to ash—a mushroom cloud

when I wake reminded I will die.
In boyhood, monsters clawed closets,
their shark-toothed snarls palpable
as my own skin. My teenage years

I never feared ghouls after punching
the bully who called me an afterbirth,
my body Beowulf teaching Grendel.
This didn't kill my dread. I merely buried

devils under sleep. Closing my eyes
the Elf King's flaming lids open.

11

Thanatophobia

I cried because life is hopeless and beautiful.
—Howard Nemerov

Earth spins, blessed by corn snakes
and measured dripping snails. I looked
at my watch in math class, and knew:
the secondhand notches closer to my death
when I'd lose my lover, the world.
Heaven, preachers said, is the reward
for goodness. Could I smell fresh mown grass
from vapored cloudy mansions?
Here, strawberries fatten like gravid spiders,
streetlamps drape night's ghosts
in blue gowns. Dread knocked my guts,
clock hands swirling to abyss
where the dead feel and want nothing,
having no self. God couldn't fashion
a richer universe than ours.
Mayflies live one day, mating
in flitting patties of wings. Dying,
they shower rivers without hope
of paradise, or lust for remembrance.
God is fleshy as mint leaves, the fissured moons
of bread rolls. The world is enough for love.

Love Song to a Harvest Mouse

I bless your harvest, your whiskers
tender as fizz. The wild trumpets of your ears
cup the wind for a rustling copperhead
that could mix your blood with venom
rotting your raspberry heart.

I can give you nothing you need,
only these words, spoken under chimneys
spicing the autumn stars.

I love your body, your pink feet
tapping grass. I crave your eyes,
the swirled cord of your tail, your prickling snout,
to tell you a billion things,
how squid gush ink in a place called the sea
and other worlds orbit other suns.

Mice live only eighteen months,
enough to learn joy
before the void devours our lives.
One day, the final flower wilts
and the last living cell freezes on Earth.

We are larger than the abyss
as I offer love simple as bread.
Home asleep, I dream of you
running gossamer meadows forever.

Ode to Snakes

Among monks and poets, the ordinary
is sexy. Oil-black garter snakes
with yellow highway stripes, ribbon earth
for grubs richer than chocolate.

Molting, their eyes are blue gumdrops,
undressing their skins, renewed
smooth as apples. Rattlesnake fangs
jab rats with witchy milk, venom

that clots blood to jelly. For the Hopi,
snakes mimic an umbilicus,
nursing people to soil. Bobbi-Bobbi,
an Australian serpent god, gave

humankind one of his ribs
for the first boomerang.
Some seekers love hallowed voids
in desolate heavens. Others

prefer rippled ropes of snakes
bellying fields for mice or mates.
The yawning moccasin holds
the whole moon in her mouth.

Bullfrog Witness

My cheeks billow yellow sacks
with words creaking like the shed door
the old man opens to my world.
The pond's nectar of minnows, clumps
of cow paddies, skies blue as damselflies

light earth's smelly circle. The old man
slashes grass, riding a red metal horse
that snarls gasoline anger.
I mushroom myself with air
to frighten water snakes

and bleat wet warnings to other males
this liquid acre is my nation.
Goats in the west pasture don't know
what I am, the neighbor's boys
ignore my heart shaped body

pluming in a green stew
to new ponds over the barbed wire.
Youths romp innocent as wild grapes
through mesquite thickets, playing chase
with sticks, dreaming human dreams.

Children grow tall with sorrows
weeping in hot buffalo grass, crisp fields
beyond my water which must be cruel.
Angry fathers have ripe red faces.
Their country is wide, yet they're not free.

Verses from Elmer

I'm a stuffed triceratops
with butterfly-soft fabric
teal as lagoons. My father
shimmers in my black eyes
while his breath ships my name.

Three ice-cream cone horns
nudge the air, my frill's shamrock
rising from my neck. Some say
I'm inanimate, though *I think,*
therefore I am—for all objects

house a soul. I love the world
for aardvarks I've not seen,
though I imagine bleat
accordion music, have seventeen eyes
and thirty snouts beyond my closet

of teddy bears. The universe
is tender. Blue ghosts wait
in the weeping wind for my father
to nurse their griefs back to joy.
I'm happy, so happy to be real.

Stray Cat

She stared when I opened the back door,
a tangerine tabby, wild as ice
on November shingles, a nutmeg tiger
stalking autumn leaves for doves.
I stepped outside, and she ran away

from human dominion, bricked houses,
trucks like gassy bulls jolting down streets.
I'm nice, I wanted to say. Let me stroke
your coat's silky flame, so you'll purr
tiny earthquakes in my hands.

I love you, I called. She stayed feral,
afraid of humanity. Who can blame her?
People shear forests, grow missile gardens
with napalm flowers. I saw my fallen shape
in her eyes where the world burned.

Worm Saviors

After childhood rainstorms, worms washed
from front yards to street curbs.
I handed those mud-eels back

to lawns where their guts packed dirt.
I still love them, thriving like rat tails
underfoot, pink noodles plowing bones

to grass. Birds bludgeon those meat-whips
that perforate the world.
I think they speak, hissing at plants,

commanding blooms, slurping prairies,
wet yarns twisting under mushrooms.
However grotesque their grimy rites,

they weave the loam's wealth for wheat
and corn, soil nursed by worms
jaunting like fish through the earth.

Arachnophilia

Eight-fingered hands, black plums of venom
under logs, spiders jot silk to the wind

where my kisses blow. I doubt they love me
in return. To orchard weavers

humans must seem Cthulhu-huge monsters
smashing their flesh to paste, so light

I can't hear their legs rasping
like dark snowflakes petting the ground.

Some dangle on webs, wrapping flies
in gossamer tortillas. Shaggy pinballs,

jumping spiders pounce on carpets,
abdomens fat with gnats and eggs,

spiderling kernels ripe for birth.
People fear those jittery grapes

yet Earth's the only world where spiders
shroud twigs in diaphanous bridal veils.

Meeting a Cottonmouth

My camera lens coils to cricket frogs
pouncing on the river. Somewhere,
cave salamanders, blind as soap
slap dripping rocks. On the trail

a fattened boomerang wriggles his tail,
his throat jammed by a rat, swallowing
prey in a glacial, reverse birth. My photo
shows the rodent's back feet plunging

through the snake. I imagine
Appalachian churchgoers shaking
armfuls of rattlers, crooning halleluiah,
the woman cradling her Gaboon viper

before the landlord finds her dead.
I love the cottonmouth, his eyes
two berries of lava, his ebony crescent
fanged white. Few friends cared for my frog,

barred owl and damselfly pictures,
but praised the water moccasin
like a soft, venomous cane, stirring
our fate mortal as the rat.

In Genesis, the serpent slid bellying
on earth, accursed by heaven,
yet his mouth's sweet canker
sends people to God.

Part II

1999

Friday night margaritas chime, toasting tomorrow's
new millennium. A jukebox serenades *kiss me*
out of the bearded barley. The drunk pool player
tells Bill Clinton sex jokes, argues Yahoo
is the best search engine. Tankards fizz beer and hope.

If sheep can be cloned, someone says, we'll have
Martian colonies, war abolished, the future bursting
to blossom with Times Square fireworks. We'll craft better songs
than Macarena, artists tapping the nectar of making.
Stars thumped heartbeats through the void, beckoning
Earth's promise, bowls ladled with plenty, cash-crammed wallets,
towers higher than Babel stacked against forever.
Neon shimmers on smiles. Nothing could go wrong.

The bar stays open in 2020. A musty heater
smells like childhood summers, gardens shafted with flaxen lilies,
long yellow grasshoppers, dust on vinyl, a favorite scarf,
a mother reading bedtime stories, her breath
softer than the rustle of a girl combing her hair.

The Big Dipper

... we came forth, and once more saw the stars.
—Dante's *Inferno*, Robert Pinksy trans.

After six hundred thousand Covid dead
in the states, I drive to a country pasture
so night frogs might cure my grief.

Fireflies glint warm shards over switchgrass
strummed by wind. No freight train bawls
in the dark for what has been or could be.

People aren't harvest mice thrashing for seeds.
We demand gifts from the universe
this azure planet can't provide. Above,

the big dipper buoys seven urchins
in the oceanic dome of space.
Only Earth houses heaven and hell.

In five billion years the sun
boils all whales of the sea to ash.
Could a mouse tolerate such terms?

I vow skyward in silent vespers
to love Earth like a bride
so the stars may remember the world.

Insta Joy

Before Facebook, YouTube, or Twitter
I harvested fossils at Benbrook Lake:
spiked crinoids and ammonite wheels
rolled from dead Cretaceous oceans.

I couldn't find one full spiral shell,
only slices of eddies, sometimes pale
and brittle, others dark and hard
like an ebony sickle. I was nine,

well into my dinosaur phase, ankylosaurs
my favorite, my yellow triceratops
Trimey won wrestling matches with teddy bears.
I lugged dregs of ammonite shards

while my dog hunted my footsteps
in friendship. Reaping parcels of beasts,
I came home, read Goosebumps' novels—
suburban yetis, krakens in deep blue.

June bugs butted porch lights like rutting rams
in love with lamps when slick fresh mown grass
perfumed the black fiddles of crickets
before the internet.

Love Poem to a Mason Jar

I find you in a garage,
genie of milk and sunrise.
Scrubbing dust from your thickness
I head outdoors to fill your flesh.

Your body opens for housing
miracles, pond scum with spiders
prancing and snails nursing mud,
tinctures of starlight, the world.

I'd impregnate you with seashells,
stew or salad, fermenting angels
closed by your clear cocoon,
your silent bell. I push moss inside

and soak the witchy broth in a spring,
slime drenched like melted frogs
bejeweled with water bears. I pack
baubles of joy into your glassy womb.

A Billion Heartbeats

As a general rule, all mammals, from mice to whales,
get a billion heartbeats over their lifetimes.
—Sam Kean, *Wall Street Journal*

A hummingbird heart spasms 1200 beats
per minute. Diving, a blue whale's heartrate

slows at two per minute, blood valved
through a meat-balloon the weight of a cow

heard two miles away. When the heart
stops, the dead fester in earth, their fleshy drums

puttered to silence. Positivists
think death is naked oblivion,

the brain's sea anemone dried like burnt wicks
in dirt, the self with it. Some ask,

why love the world if there's heaven?
All goodnight kisses, dogs chasing their tails

and each pleasure jaunts between the revving
and rotting of the heart's hot plum,

clouds so dappled with birds, the void
is an impossible death sentence.

Can happiness pulse inside the coffin?
What's eternity? – grapes clustered

in chilled green blimps, inchworms throbbing
on rhubarbs, coffee's black nectar,

a new car smelling like clay, breath
measured by beating apples in our chests.

Ode to Pill Bugs

Tiny log-lobsters, their antennae
kiss dead ferns, reaping
crumbled blooms to dirt
where the pink worm judders
below roots' tender whips.

I love their egg-shaped tractors,
their armor rolled to leggy globes.
I bless their eyelash-feet,
damp nunneries champing leaflitter,
pilgrims seeking sodden wood.

Crawling mud-monks, they nibble
the tallest redwood back to crumbs.
Their humble ovals seek
no power or glory,
only the renewal of spring.

Dear Razorback Musk Turtle

Sun butters your carapace, ridged
in a gothic arch. Did you know the sun
is a star? – a nuclear fusion foundry
smelting elements, hellscapes soothed to grass.

Basking, your eyes' poppyseeds
blotted with caution from my approach.
I didn't mean to drive you back
to water, dark cologne steaming from your scutes,

sweet brother of ruptured stars. Where you live,
downy woodpeckers hack live oaks, troves
of ruby crowned kinglets spatter the blue
with wings. Can you hear the chickadees?

I don't know what you think of anoles
flaunting their throat's pink flags. I'm sorry
milk jugs and beer cans spoil your waters.
I only hope you bite fat apple snails,

you want nothing besides mossy pleasure
with love pure as rain sowing willows
in teary seeds, and alone you aren't lonely,
shy dinosaur, my tender moonrock.

Can you hear the nightly trains rambling
over the creek bridge, calling into
this same hatched universe, this star-born body?
Where are we from? Where are we going? Home.

Dirt Ecstasies

Imagine a hell boring as Kansas,
cattle trucks rattling freeways
with belching hogs or heifers,
dentist waiting rooms and parking lots.

When no one looks, office pencils dance.
The abandoned schoolyard lies pregnant
with angels. Salads swirl galaxies
of ranch dressing and crouton moons.

Consider the electricity of stale cheese.
Raindrops are ghosts' wet thumbprints.
Even in Kansas, a thousand earthworms
quake through an acre of dirt.

Deer Skull

Beyond suburbs, your jaw sleeps
under wind-threshed flails of woodoats.
Ants search the wild kernels

of your teeth. Your brain melts to dirt;
your hooves' dark plums shrivel
and sprout mistflowers. Once,

your door-slender body leapt
over guardrails, crossing highways
through hellish eggs of headlights.

Perhaps no one remembers you
nuzzling autumn hoarfrost,
printing clay with steps gentle

as ghostberries. Your bones bloom
like cocoons into wings. All flesh
hatches an infinite spring.

The Violence of Flowers

Gänseblümchen, German for daisy, or geese-flower.
Under clear Tokyo skies, cherry blossoms flower

buttercream stars in spring. Titan arum smells
of rotten meat, growing a twelve-foot flower.

Almost nothing bloomed between Jurassic ferns.
Sauropods slogged bread-dark earth before flowers

erupted, butterflies plundering nectar lush
as cantaloupes, dragging pollen, guzzling flowers.

Oleanders open soft pink blades, poisonous
as a witch's salad, or nightshade's deadly flower.

April storms slather pastures. Lightning flogs
sprouting oaks—cars slurped by a tornado's flower

before bluebonnets lance from dirt, loam mixed
with milled bones, corpses churned into flowers.

Deer Shall Inherit the Earth

Back from Christmas, the plane skims
Des Moines' snow-sugared runway,
the sky gray as nails. Midnight,

the shuttle comes. Winds hack my face
bared to the New Year, bags hauled inside.
Streetlamps glow ghostly hulks over cornfields

from broken tallgrass prairie, riding north
to Ames on 35, earth bright
as a fallen angel's corpse.

A fever rasps my throat while I think
of this country's death. America
sprang like maize from the wilderness.

Her husk disrobed golden fruit, her tassels
wilting bitter to the dirt. Maybe
a nation built on murder and slaving

was never a new Jerusalem.
All empires end, even this world one day
will spin brown and treeless in the void.

The van reaches Ames where deer haunt
the snow with elfin measure.
A doe walks noiseless as clouds, the ground

caressed by hooves so tender
they barely crack spokes of snowflakes.
She bows her heard for dry forbs, her neck

ballerina slender. Her breath fogs
warm phantoms at the city's fringe,
her tribe older than ours, her eyes'

black planets watching and waiting
for another human society
to founder into white ruins. The van

reaches the station, night's darkness huge
and lonely. Deer live their whole lives
without speaking. They have no names.

Breaking Bread

Sourdough, naan, pumpernickel,
grain-born loaves swaddled like babies
sleep on supermarket shelves.
Ten thousand years ago, flatbreads
cooked over Levant campfires, metates,
Mesoamerican grinding stones
still chaff-stained. The homeless fish
dumpsters to find bread buttered
with mold as sailors nibbled
maggot-riddled biscuits called hardtacks.
Witch trials, convulsing women
deemed possessed, ate fungus-rancid rye,
black goats clouding their acid trips.

Desert foxes raised one feral boy
who wandered to Las Cruces,
kissed by a drunk streetwalker, her mouth
the odor of wet dough. He remembered
his human mother, her sweetbread-breath
humid at midnight, her arms
gentle as baguettes the morning
a housefire baked his family.

God's body breaks among lovers
and enemies. The orphan viewed
the desert from his mental ward's window,
his speech foxy yips and growls.
Nurses gave him bagels for breakfast.
His mouth voiced no words. Only bread.

Adam Means Red Earth

> There is nothing to eat,
>   seek it where you will,
>   but of the body of the Lord.
>   —William Carlos Williams

Outside Sweetwater, bones roast
into rosy clay. Plains sweep past
the freeway like unleavened bread.
Butchers conjure dark eucharists,
Herefords slaughtered for steak wafers.

The pickup's tire ruptures, swerving
head-on to the opposite lane.
The charcoal-blackened wreck kindles
flames smelting plastic to steel,
a smore of death, boiling marrow.

Jackrabbits listen with ladling ears
the whistle of big rig trailers,
headlights coiling through darkness,
a tortilla moon baked in night's griddle
of stars. The police processed

nine killed, most in their twenties.
Their parents' eyelashes are tear-thickened wicks.
A mile off the highway, crickets carol
in a crumbled adobe chapel,
fiddling legs in parched fonts

where holy water pooled. The dead
pierce the living's dreams, ghosts
steamed through air vents, their kingdom
made from memory and earth.
Ashes to ashes, dust to dust.

Linear A

Bullfrogs squawk like mud-trumpets.
One study found prairie dogs chirp
warnings for women in yellow shirts.

Cro-Magnons painted twisting auroch horns
but no one knows their names.
Most words are lost among bones

or not called words by linguists.
Jellyfishes' gelatinous bells
gleam a calligraphy of light.

Who are people to deny lines of ants
speaking pheromones, tasting
acid glyphs juiced in dirt?

Minoans of bronze age Crete leapt
over bulls, worshipped snake goddesses,
wrought octopi on pithoi. Earthquakes

punctured eardrums, clay tablets milled
to dust all tongues become. Their script,
Linear A, remains undeciphered

as humpbacked whales bawling hymns,
wolves' hornsong vowels, an owl feeding
her chicks with mice rich as language.

The Making

> *...the caterpillar digests itself, releasing enzymes to dissolve all of its tissues. If you were to cut open a cocoon or chrysalis at just the right time, caterpillar soup would ooze out.*
> —Ferris Jabr, *Scientific American*

The night park is lonely
as snails sledding pavement.
A plastic bag catches ghosts
and the cocoon snags a twig.

Juicy cells chant DNA
rosaries. Grass grows like breath,
sunlight bewitched into sugar.
Drainpipes drip mossy sticks

rattling on straws and cups.
Moth-flesh thickens, her heart's jelly
pinging blood through her
brainy ganglion. Beer bottles roll

dead cisterns without the spell
of making. Moonflowers open
white gowns of ripened pollen,
the world spins beyond permission

or desire, and the moth breaks
her dangling coffin, her wings
clapping yellow applause.

Elegy to the Ivory-Billed Woodpecker

*As of today, the U.S. Fish and Wildlife Service (FWS)
has made its position known: The agency has proposed
officially removing the Ivory-billed Woodpecker from
the endangered species list and declaring the iconic
woodpecker extinct.*
—Andrew Del-Colle, *Audubon Magazine*

I pray you still live,
flame-crested bird
netted through bald cypress twigs,
feathered black like a mad deacon
in a church of owls,
hacking hardwoods with your cream-white beak
for your last webworm caterpillar
succulent as Earth.

My lament can't make your bones sing
clarinet notes through gator-lazy swamps,
mosses' green gumbo bobbing
with punctured barrels and shopping carts.

Crawdads sob in hot lagoons.
Plovers whistle griefs where hurricanes
cry salt tears from the gnashing wind.
Powerlines snap, spiders wrap
woodsheds in silk funeral shrouds, yet you
my friend, have not come back.

When rain stops, a clear sky weeps
meteors. Spring hatchlings crack open-mouthed
from eggs. New birds evolve, though never again
will your love song trumpet through the trees.

Beasts Naming Adam

Silence begets words; words beget silence.
Frog throats billow in a boggy gumbo.
Sugar ants taste chemical glyphs

on the linoleum floor, spelling
the dog's kibble. Lanternfish speak
syllables of light, blackness candled

in lapis halos. Hogs belch phrases
for swill and love, snouts signifying
the world's presence. Dawn choruses,

birds lullaby their eggs, new wings
slurring through yolk. The first humans
heard the lion thunder like a god

commanding sunrise. Meerkats stirred
from mazy humps of earth to name
this anonymous biped, who, in turn,

christened each creeper and mover,
doves cooing through mist, seashells
whispering surf, water, stars,

grass, rocks, past, present, and futures
milling bones back to red dust
that birthed Adam. Before galaxies

fronded from the void, before moon or rain,
the naked abyss waited
in silence for singing to begin.

Ghost Tracks

Urban legend assumes that in 1930s San Antonio, Texas,
a train collided with a school bus, killing 10 children.
Visitors still park at the alleged crash site to sprinkle
baby powder on their cars. Some report seeing small
handprints on their powdered vehicles.

Children played "I spy with my little eye"
but none saw the train punch the bus.

Side panels punctured like a stabbed can of beans,
ragged swords of glass and steel splitting
apart its guts, still-birthing children on gravel
as the train gored deeper in the wounded bus
like an enraged industrial bull, hellsmoke
sneezed from his chimney, blowlamps of his eyes
blazing into night thronged with milksnakes,
raccoons shocked by the booming slap of metal
until nothing but silence,

the children seeing their misted spirits seethe
like fog from their bones and new wispy hands
but this was their final hallucination
before death, no fingerprints pressing
from their remains and no afterlife,
the world holding the dead inside her,
the violent deliverance of flowers,
holy Earth twisting her blue speck, the only home
for birds and falling in love
where the dead aren't ghosts but grass
and bottleflies greener than Elysium

while the children saw for their last hot second
grackle-peppered powerlines swaying
with lightning current, the great horned owl
roosting on a live oak outside Boerne,
the Milky Way splashed over Fredericksburg,
one millisecond slowing down to drink
with their vision the world's radiance,
a grand procession of snails purpling eyestalks,

40

the children happy their final blip is heaven
beyond time they've inherited, the universe
unfettered from flesh like a soul
and the unchained rainbow spumes free.

Part III

Space Hogs

> So long as the void Is hysterical…
> —James Dickey, The Moon Ground

Snouts moonward, weightless hooves batter
starlight in a rocket that spears the void.

Blue Earth glimmers on their tongues,
Africa's shape blazing with whipped cream clouds.

The pigs don't know where they are, why
they tumble through air like flying loaves.

Where's pungent mud, the humid nectar
of swill? Perhaps farmers or some pig god

thieved heft from the ground, turned bellies
to balloons, sow teats to bubbles,

tails to noodles. Shoats try suckling
but drift towards the ceiling port

where galactic light roils planets
richer than whale milk. They try rubbing

themselves awake from their oozing dream
but keep floating in the black river

of stars. They pray for rescue, grunting
and squealing, God's silenced pealed

in their sailing ears, their sounds, the abyss
speaking. The universe oinks.

Voyage to Pluto

My favorite "planet" as a boy,
Pluto hung like a bead threaded
in two-hundred-year orbits,
treading darkness with its snowberry.

I dreamed it held wooly mammoths.
Translucent walruses loafed on its moon,
oceans of icebergs and krakens.
2015, New Horizons revealed Pluto,

undressing its round body from the void,
baring mountains and chasms the first time
like a naked angel for human eyes.
In boyhood, I wanted to colonize

its frost with my dog and hamster,
christen a country of kindness.
I'd lodge stuffed animals in my space ark,
pilot the black frontier and build

a nation whose motto is Love.
Here I am, far away on a planet
dripping with grapes and people
who've forgotten to cherish this world.

Ohthere the Astronaut

Walrus in Old English is *horshwæl*.
Ohthere journeyed to Norway's north coast
in King Alfred's time and found horsey whales

pulsing on beaches like blubbery grubs
tusked with moonlight, chonky balloons
chomping fish-heads. Ohthere

did not discover walruses; the Sami
named them, and before people,
laughing gannets and polar bears

found these tender boats of fat
loafing seaward. One day space aliens
may "discover" us, a tentacled Ohthere

from the glittering celestial vacuum,
a purple squid helmed in a spacesuit.
Is he a god, devil, or envoy?

Will Ohthere's kind colonize the world
or offer friendship? Earth's blueberry
is ripe for picking and plunder.

Beaches bright with seawood beckon
intimate as flesh, stranger than angels,
shimmering curlews calling home.

Outside Monahans

Windmills like sunflowers rattle
when storms ferment over Monahans.
Udders of clouds lactate lightning and rain.
Here, a pastor killed himself
thirty years ago. His wife never tells
their daughter her father's name.
All love is holy, the reverend announced
before the church removed him.
God made me gay and beautiful.

Heavenward, angels shake trailers
with dust baths, the dead crying thunder
across the desert. His daughter
tastes his praise in the wind.

The Millennial Folksinger

Driving southwest through badlands,
wind strums the grass, sunrise bleeding
my guitar strings red, Kansas prairies
springing from murdered tribes and bison skulls.

My throat spools music, my banjo
rambling through Denver and Vegas
where I yip Woody Guthrie,
Leadbelly and Dylan covers.

My voice blows gospels, delivering
the poor from prison, to lasso heaven
onto Earth. I feed revelations
for the language-famished who've chewed

bumper sticker slogans. My songs
fill listeners like bread, God's body
leavened into lyrics. My guitar thunders
over the Rockies, yet I've no money

save for busking on stage as the rich
get richer. Each dawn the world rolls
closer to death, forest fires
wreathing the sun in funeral shrouds.

I sing for a business charity dinner:
*I'd hammer out justice, I'd hammer out
a warning* and nothing happens
except me growing older.

Let There Be Light

From space, blue earth glimmers
blessed by hooves. No other world
has lovemaking and blackberries.
Everybody who lived, lives here.

Zoom to suburbs one April night.
A lone cricket rings in flickering grass.
Sheet-shawled sleepers dream
their late grandfather's face
genuine as clay. Others dream
of baseball, their first school dance. Light comes

so white it x-rays the rooms. Cars stall
on freeways. A mushroom cloud climbs;
downtown cinders to incense

as cobs in shucks blast to popcorn,
wallpaper crisps like peeled skin,
deranged angels smearing fire through hands
of sweetgum leaves, Old Testament wrath
on fresh mown lawns where the family dog barks
and does not understand.

Afterlife

Captain Wumpushead, my frog, died of dropsy
cramming his stomach like a mashed plum.
Lighting the fishtank, I fed him bloodworms
he nipped in stabbing gulps. Sometimes Captain
missiled up the tank for air, then dove
underwater again. He lived five years
and his absence presses my brain
with the tender ferns of his claws.

I still think he's veiled in the wisteria
to thrust forward with his torso's nimble grape.
I don't believe in ghosts or heaven
or know if a frog understands friendship
on human terms. His whisking heartbeat
became the wild prayer of the world.
Wherever I go, his love settles
patiently in water, waiting for me.

A Garden Slug has 27,000 Microscopic Teeth

The last snow froths among gutters
bitter as cankers mixed with oil.
Loam-made bones sweat ghosts
dallying through low pools of fog.
Downtown, skyscrapers like great tusks
jut from the gumline of cement.
My dentist pulls a bad wisdom tooth.
I nurse my palate's bruised plum,
swishing saltwater after eating. Spring
comes in two weeks, my tooth buried
under muddy wood. Garden slugs
chomp moss in slurping rasps
to dirt for yellow prairie broomweed.
Soggy angels complete my flesh.

The Fermi Paradox

*The Drake equation estimates the number of spacefaring
extraterrestrials. Estimates range from over a thousand
to one million alien civilizations living in the Milky
Way. That none have been found or contacted the
Earth, despite their high probability of existing, is
called the Fermi Paradox.*

San Antonio, I walk the river bars.
A mariachi band thunders guitars,
bawling mournful ballads
this dough-warm night. Moon,

take my hand in your bridal light.
Cosmos, bring me alien ships from depths
telling me humanity might survive
its mania for missiles and mansions.

Dinosaurs, the dodo, extinct ghosts
gnash muffled griefs in the void,
stars and planets glugged by black holes
slurping the abyss. Through speakers,

Hank Williams croons freight train vowels:
his lonesome elegy to love,
to lips soft as birds, kissing
mutual language without words.

Rabbits whisk over brambles.
Sheep wool curls like hot threads of straw.
Sparrows sing that Earth isn't lonely.
The world is a voice from the stars.

Other

*In Hebrew, the word for Holy, kadosh, means separate,
other. And sometimes it's the very otherness of a
stranger...can jerk us out of our habitual selfishness,
and give us intonations of that sacred otherness which
is God.*
—Karen Armstrong, interview with Bill Moyers

Why take them to our leader? Should aliens
land in Washington or London
to greet heads of state, or visit nomads
in Mongolia? One moonless hour
white spheres bubbled over the snow-heaped
Altai mountains. Asleep in her yurt,
Bolarmaa, a shepherdess woke to thunder
under clear heaven, stars boiling
in night's black brew. Orion's belt
gained a fourth sun fallen to grassy steppes.
A lucent pillar of light speared earth
and let purple tendrilled space slugs
enter the world like seraphim to Isaiah
saying: *kadosh, kadosh, kadosh,*
holy, holy, holy, and other.

Instead of words, the gelatinous angels
"talked" like ants, spitting and tasting pheromones.
Bolarmaa dropped to her knees in prayer.
Cinnamon musk pierced the air
in hazy spices. Maternal care seized her
when the odor spoke: the universe
is sacred. All birds are blessed, black holes, camels,
galaxies, birth, life, death, hallowed and affirmed.

Otherness came from the sky
to meet like strangers fallen in love.
Speak to me, lovers say, perfume me
with your body's taste.
Oh God yes, oh God Yes.

The Ontology of Prairie Dogs

Why is there something rather than nothing?
—Leibniz, *Monadology*

Why is the color green real?
Prairie dogs stand like tiny grizzlies.
Squirreling sod-gnomes, no other
galaxy contains their gourd-round bellies.

Their musk seethes through spring fog.
Pups nurse white syrups of milk,
native plains ninety-five percent paved,
tilled, poisoned. Everything burns

with this same cosmos, a mown lawn
smelling hot as hay sopping
a horse's back, grasshoppers
shredding portholes in eggplant leaves,

the biscuit moon's basalt, sweet rolls
laced with eddies of snaily icing,
prairie dogs made from ruptured stars,
merging into what never dies.

Clownfish in Love with the Moon

My carnival mouth slurps
specks of fairy shrimp.
I want to kiss the white squid
swimming in the sky, her tendrils
of light filed through scallops,
candling the creature inside.
I'll leave my home of polyps
to press her warm mantle
creaming my tangerine lips.

The Ecstasy of Owls

The sleep
Of reason is not darkness, but another kind of light.
—Sophocles, from *Antigone*, Don Taylor trans.

The owl gazes from an oak,
his clockwork face grandfathered
in wood. When the park closes

for visitors, the barred owl murders
the wind, whisking to powerlines,
clasping and slurping a vole.

To make an owl, one must multiply
infinity by mottled twigs,
spells of unreason, beak,

talon, and nightly queries,
Who cooks for you? hooted
to the moon's hammock.

Naming the darkness between planets,
he glides the wordless country
before birth, after death, beyond

jade jungles with undiscovered frogs,
white shingles of polar caps.
His wings blaze like gossamer fire

from burst stars where grass spurs
in terrible pleasure, and the world
turns in the black cherries of his eyes.

Rumpelstiltskin

...with rage, he grabbed his foot with both hands, and
ripped himself in half.
—Translation from the 1857 Brothers Grimm version

My name glows inside my brain
spoken by blind mares. Glittering roots
taste my appellation's syllables.
The miller's daughter cannot whisper
my curse, damning my bones to dust.

My body precedes speech.
Unwritten stars must not spell
their flames in the deep,
worms strumming through loam
pulsing wordless music.

I unname the universe,
swallows whistling without branding
rafter, lamppost, moonlight.
If someone pilfers my identity
from the sunless seabed, the otter's throat,

I'll grab my foot to tear my torso
in half, my name like a fox
tumbling through a yellow glade
among birdsong, wind, and rain.
I become the world.

If the Moon were Human

The moon knows unspeakable pleasure.
If she were a ferret, she'd scurry
snow-footed from haybales to the sea,

dipping the tide's melodious stairs. If she
were dough, bakers would scroll her luminous back
into gull-bright bread, her body

leavened for butter-syllabled mouths.
If the moon were a book, she'd teach
an encyclopedia of craters with pages

stony and white. Pregnant with milk,
cream or nutmeg, her nectar
nurses bats, blonding harvest wheat,

thickening silkworms' straw-yellow cocoons.
If the moon were human, she'd sing
her lonely pursuit of dawn, her tongue

stirring night's clouds, lyrics drowned
by crooning lovesick dogs. She'd bless
this bitter void of stars, her hair undone

in grass. Her blue throat would lullaby
weeping children, homeless men splashing
in her hands. If the moon were human.

Life Stew

Boil saline puddles of ash, spiced
with yellow sulfur. Mix
lightning bolts and cyanide salts
to a paste of carbon. Brew
ammonia and methane, fermented
to a mash of sour soot. Grate
meteor crumbs with volcanic grime,
a fiesta from fetid slop, sugars
smelted to the riving wisps
of a double helix. Let the stew
simmer until DNA ladders build
trilobite eyes, wild green eels, humans
painting the Sistine Chapel, witnessing
the universe that sees itself.

Black Hole Singing

*In 2022, NASA transferred a black hole's pressure
waves to an audio file. This sonification provided
listeners with sounds 250 million light years distant.*

My first one-night stand, she freed
her skin from the silk cocoon
of her dress, our lovemaking
more mechanical than expected.
I remember her beehive breasts

and her womb's humid chapel
before we listened to the dry air.
We heard immense clocks swirl,
bomb-bright suns blinded down
a void. We lay on the bed

and clasped the pillowed lights
of our flesh. I had to leave,
so we kissed goodbye. Driving home
under broiling stars, a black hole
moaned like a freight train

almost bone-tender in the dark
lawns of junipers and spring grass.
Galaxies coiled vast choirs
though my heartbeat lullabied
a midnight quiet as the moon.

Galileo

Stirring the cullet slops, molten glass
simmers to hellish puddings of zinc
or boric oxide, the devil's tincture
casted in molds. Lenses cooled and ground
are rammed down a lead pipe. Light chokes
and bounces off a mirror made from tin,
copper and arsenic. Finished,
the telescope illumines Saturn's rings,
the Milky Way like a cluster of angels,
the pewter nimbus of the stars.

The Lake Worth Child

*In 1914, the city of Fort Worth, Texas dammed the
Trinity River, creating Lake Worth. The reservoir
covers the grave of a child.*

Wind spooled bluestem
yarned like Mamma's hair
where moles plugged earth.

Towhees stared chokecherry eyes
when I died my second April.
Fish blabbed over my sleep

after the river drowned
the church's steeple in root stew.
Bass mouths opened craters,

my tombstone's name rubbed
by snails, dreams oozing
from the soaked bones in my casket.

I remember cornbread meals
before the lake pickled pastures,
my doughy infant hands,

the wagon wheel rotting out back
where my first words cooed like a dove.
The world is deeper than waters.

Your Hands

I love you kneading your kitten's back
when she purrs little thunders,
how veins roam through your wrist
like wild eskers.

Your mushroom-touch summons April
through my blood, and your voice
clobbers ice to bluebonnets
as you sing in the street.

Stray dogs huff springtime
on your breath, your hair tasseling darkness
strumming your guitar
when the moon fructifies my dreams.

I crave your throat's lilting hymn
against the freight train's lullaby.
Your grape-tender lips chant
a prayer to the Earth

that the sun won't dissolve,
no curse salts the sap of pine trees,
and the whole world remains safe
in the breadbasket of your hands.

Getting High with You

I don't smoke weed. My favorite shrooms
are portabella. I get high
off your nails' pallid almonds,
your voice slurring half-asleep

for a glass of water. Even your tears
pull me to you, the hot salt of your grief
brings me beyond my body
where your eyes become my eyes.

I crave the mundane: parking lot grackles,
suburban squirrels, your breath
winnowing when I wake beside you,
your kisses fermenting my blood to vodka.

I follow your earthly sacraments,
moving your cat from the Christmas tree
and your dog licking between us,
our lives a tender explosion.

Bringing your plate of scrambled eggs
to bed you say, Thank you baby,
and I stagger drunk on your hair,
stoned by existence, forever.

Philosophy is Preparation for Death

Socrates said in the Phaedo. I'll die
in battle like a Viking, except I'd fight

the fear of death, my brain wrestling
my skull's crumbling theatre.

I'd hold a teddy bear, not a sword,
my Valhalla, the loam's birthday cake.

The more I love the world, the less
I believe in heaven, nothing

richer than lizards, or winged thimbles
of beetles. I'll die dancing, my jazzy knees

clanging, an old toddler
spinning in a yellow meadow,

calling kindness between all moles
celled among grubs, snakes, or Falstaff

who babbled of green fields.
My death becomes a second birth,

to face my ashes playing with dinosaurs
and sandboxes. One day, the void summons

me from my bread-hot deathbed
when snowfall cankers cow pastures,

my breath empties, and childhood
boils between my ears, lost

to infinite black space. My blood
belongs to Earth. I'll die in love with love.

Becoming the Song

Hearing is widely thought to be the last sense to go in
the dying process.
—Erik Rolfsen

Senses blending, I hear smells
and light thumping darkness
like immense sails catching wind.
Outside the hospice window, chickadees
rattle alarms for hawks. Higher,

a plane chimes the sky's cirrus-marbled bell.
Ghosts of barn owls whisk from shingles,
blueness thinning to black
until Earth grinds her orbit.
Aluminum slabs of space litter

fizz white noise across the moon. Saturn's rings
groove like records as I fly
to stars singing their chorus.
The swan-bright Milky Way swirls
curdles of static.

Galaxies bejewel the deep,
some spiraled, others spuming eggs
or bridal veils of vapor,
superclusters in spiderwebs
laced together, gossamer strings

strummed by a nameless bow.
Receded light whispers dust
and silence funnels down my ears.
Someone says goodnight and goodnight.

The Feral Child's Ecstasy

Chained in a Kansas basement, the toddler
hears hooves and horse breath swish
through bluestem. His father plunges drunk
down the stairs, keys dropped to the soiled mattress.
Unlocking himself, the boy tiptoes outside

to wind-flagged elms, sunset's spiderweb
of molten silk, the tallgrass prairie
an unfurled sheet of dough stamped
with hickory and hackberries.
He mimics the neighbors' Herefords

spooling mist from their nostrils, bawling
a meaning that speaks beyond language.
Grass rasps when thunderheads blow
mad brains of lightning and rain sings
 into earth, mixing worms and roots

of brown-eyed Susans. The child sees
the sun smelted under the plains
where murmuring angels vibrate his feet,
all holies wrapped in that slow explosion:
the cosmos that cannot be spoken, only praised.

Eric Fisher Stone is a poet and writing tutor from Fort Worth, Texas. He received his MFA in writing and the environment from Iowa State University. His poetry has appeared in numerous journals. His other full-length collections of poetry include *The Providence of Grass*, from Chatter House Press, and *Animal Joy*, from WordTech Editions.